Christmas Piano Solos
For All Piano Methods
LEVEL 4

Table of Contents

Christmas Piano Solos Level 4 is designed for use with the fourth book of any piano method.

Concepts in *Christmas Piano Solos Level 4:*

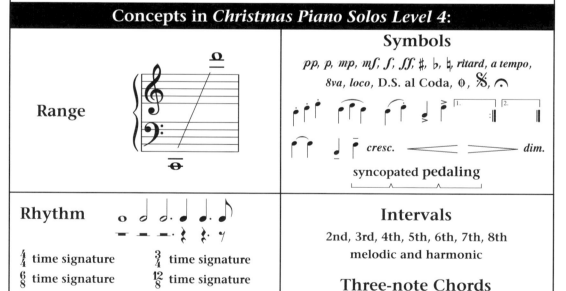

Range

Symbols

pp, p, mp, mf, f, ff, ♯, ♭, ♮, *ritard, a tempo, 8va, loco,* D.S. al Coda, ⊕, 𝄋, 𝄐

cresc. — *dim.*

syncopated pedaling

Rhythm

4/4 time signature   3/4 time signature
6/8 time signature   12/8 time signature
¢ cut time   swing eighths and syncopation

Intervals

2nd, 3rd, 4th, 5th, 6th, 7th, 8th
melodic and harmonic

Three-note Chords

blocked and broken

ISBN 978-0-7935-8580-9

HAL•LEONARD®

Visit Hal Leonard Online at
www.halleonard.com

Contact us:
Hal Leonard
7777 West Bluemound Road
Milwaukee, WI 53213
Email: info@halleonard.com

In Europe, contact:
Hal Leonard Europe Limited
42 Wigmore Street
Marylebone, London, W1U 2RN
Email: info@halleonardeurope.com

In Australia, contact:
Hal Leonard Australia Pty. Ltd.
4 Lentara Court
Cheltenham, Victoria, 3192 Australia
Email: info@halleonard.com.au

Silver Bells

from the Paramount Picture THE LEMON DROP KID

Words and Music by Jay Livingston
and Ray Evans

Joyfully

Angels We Have Heard On High

Allegretto

19th Century French Carol

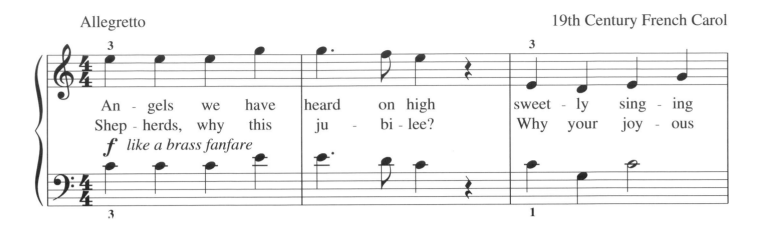

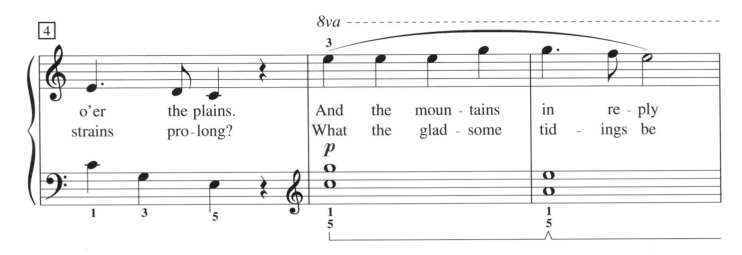

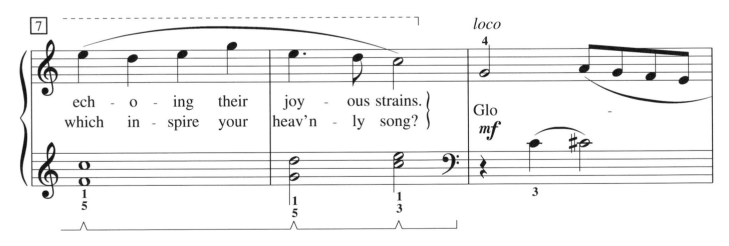

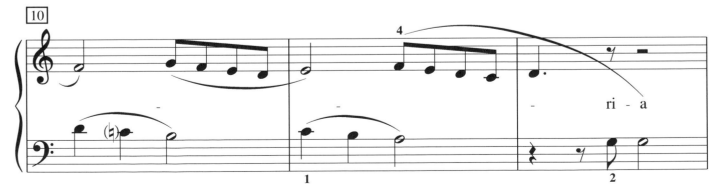

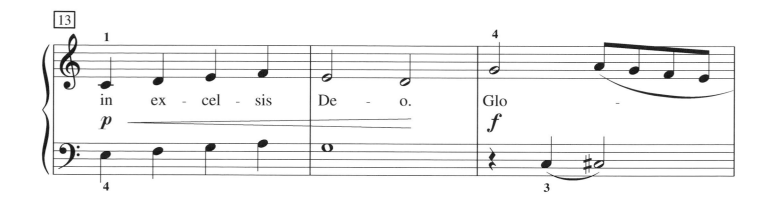

in ex - cel - sis De - o. Glo -

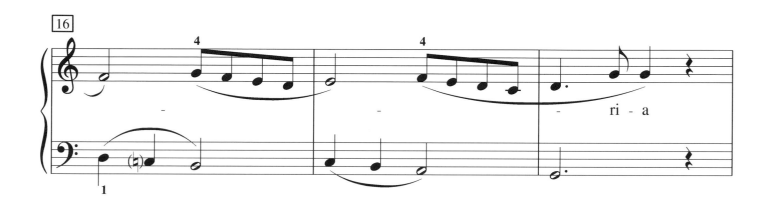

- - ri - a

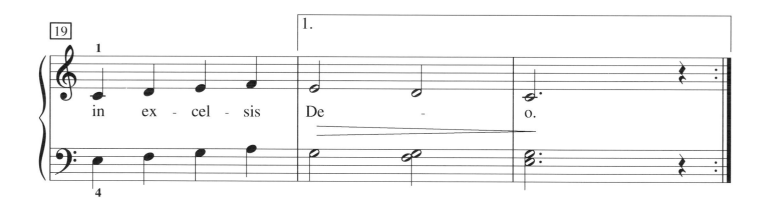

1.

in ex - cel - sis De - o.

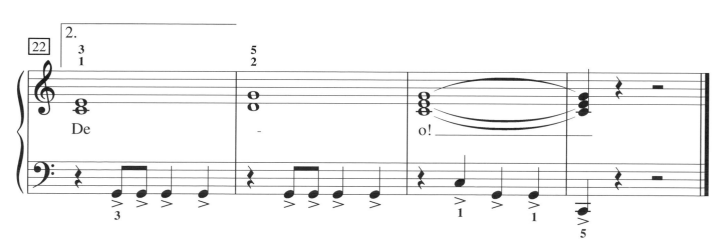

2.

De - o!

Joy To The World

Words by Isaac Watts
Music by George F. Handel

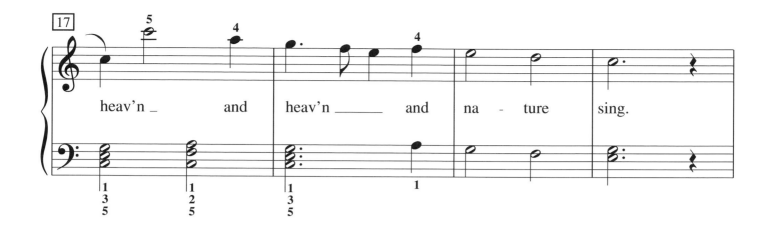

heav'n __ and heav'n _____ and na - ture sing.

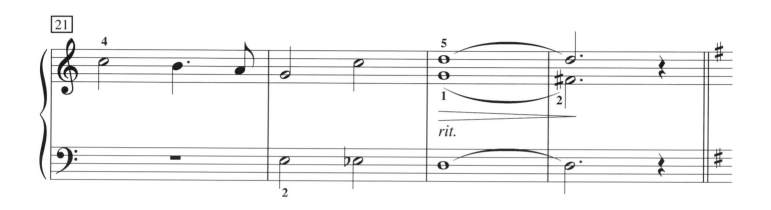

rit.

Joy to the world! The Sa - vior reigns; let

f
a tempo

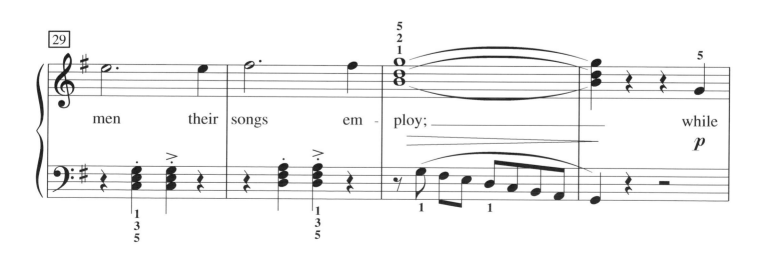

men their songs em - ploy; _____ while

p

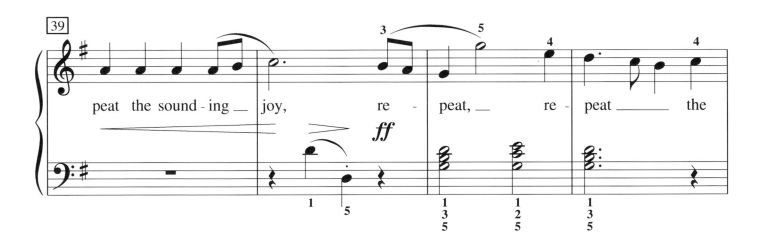

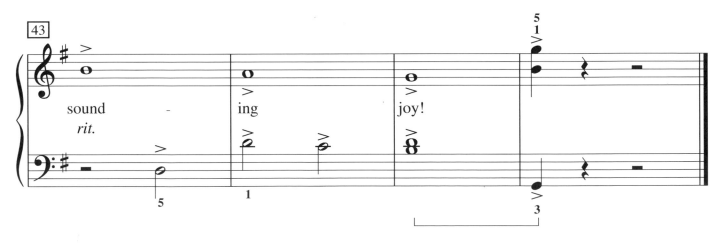

Parade Of The Wooden Soldiers

English Lyrics by Ballard MacDonald
Music by Leon Jessel

In strict march tempo

now they are near - ing, there's the cap - tain stiff as starch.

Bay - o - nets flash - ing, mus - ic is crash - ing, as the wood - en

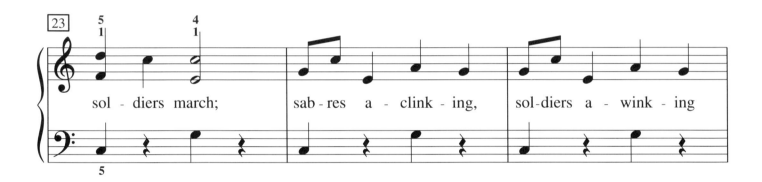

sol - diers march; sab - res a - clink - ing, sol-diers a - wink - ing

at each pret - ty lit - tle maid. Here they come! Here they come!

f

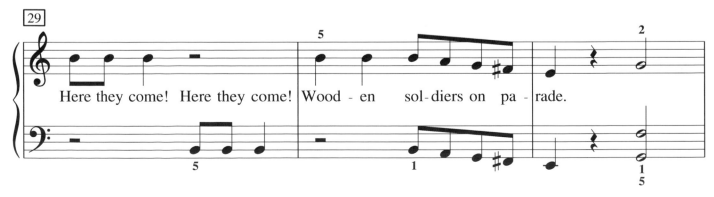

Here they come! Here they come! Wood - en sol-diers on pa - rade.

Hark! The Herald Angels Sing

Words by Charles Wesley
Music by Felix Mendelssohn-Bartholdy

Joyfully

Joy - ful all ye na - tions rise; ___ join the tri - umph
p growing louder gradually, like bells approaching from afar . . . .

of the skies; ___ with an - gel - ic host pro - claim,

"Christ is ___ born in Beth - le - hem." Hark! The her - ald

an - gels sing, "Glo - ry ___ to the new - born

King!"

The Holly And The Ivy

Gently

18th Century English Carol

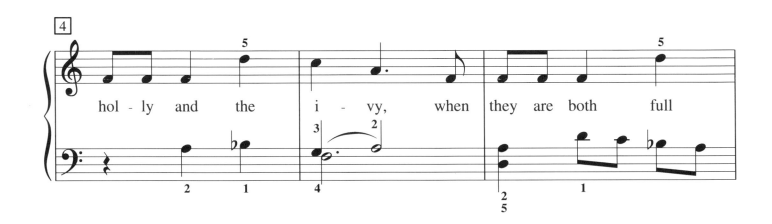

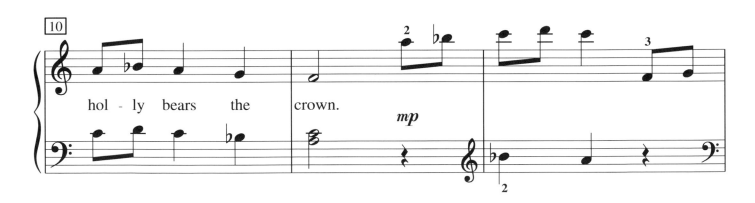

Jingle-Bell Rock

Words and Music by Joe Beal
and Jim Boothe

rock the night a - way.   Jin-gle- bell   time   is   a   swell   time,

to   go   glid-in'   in   a   one - horse   sleigh.   Gid-dy - ap,   jin - gle horse,

pick up your   feet,   jin-gle a - round   the   clock.

Mix   and   min-gle   in   a   jin - gl - in'   beat,   that's   the   Jin - gle - Bell,

that's   the   Jin - gle - Bell,   that's   the   Jin - gle - Bell   Rock.

(There's No Place Like)
Home For The Holidays

Words by Al Stillman
Music by Robert Allen

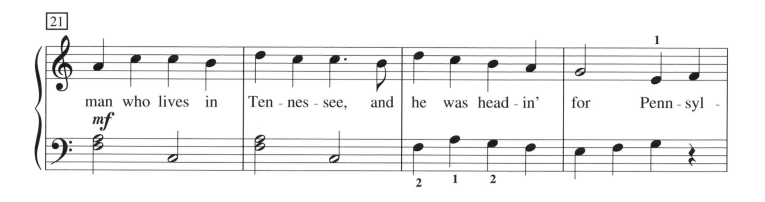

man who lives in Ten - nes - see, and he was head - in' for Penn - syl -

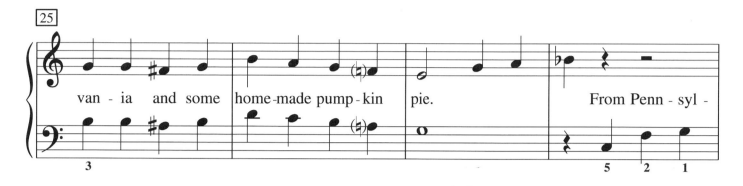

van - ia and some home-made pump - kin pie. From Penn - syl -

van - ia folks are trav - 'lin' down to Dix - ie's sun - ny shore. From At -

D.S. al Coda

lan - tic to Pa - ci - fic, gee, the traf - fic is ter - ri - fic. Oh, there's

CODA

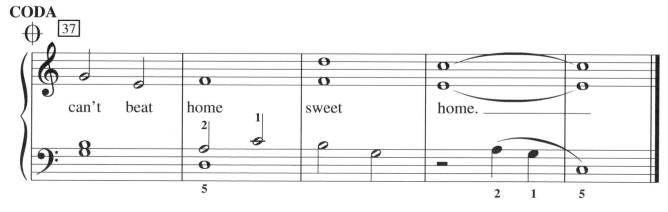

can't beat home sweet home. _____

A Holly Jolly Christmas

Some - bod - y waits for you, kiss her once for me. Have a

hol - ly jol - ly Christ-mas, and in case you did-n't hear,

oh, by gol - ly, have a hol - ly jol - ly Christ - mas

this year.

Feliz Navidad

Music and Lyrics by
Jose Feliciano

Lively Latin beat

Feliz Navidad. Feliz Navidad. Feliz Navi-dad. Pros-pe-ro a-ño y fe-li-ci-dad. Feliz Navi- I want to wish you a Mer-ry Christ-mas,

March Of The Toys

Spirited March tempo

By Victor Herbert

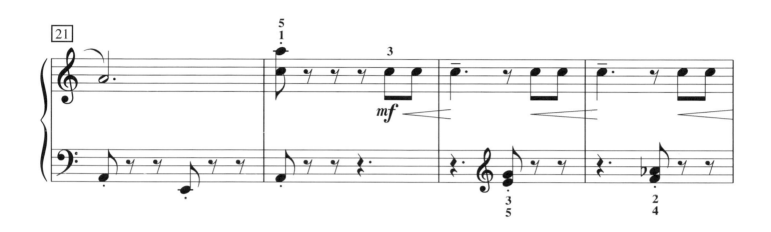

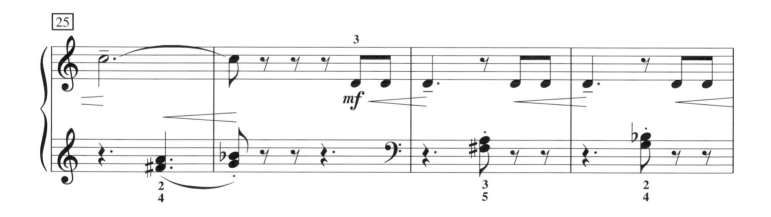

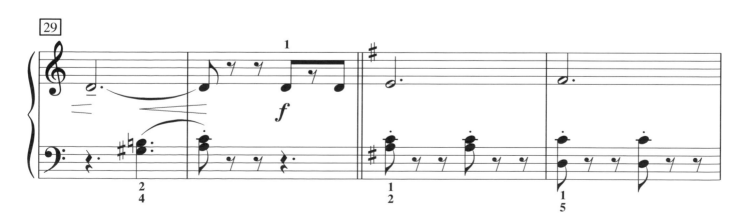

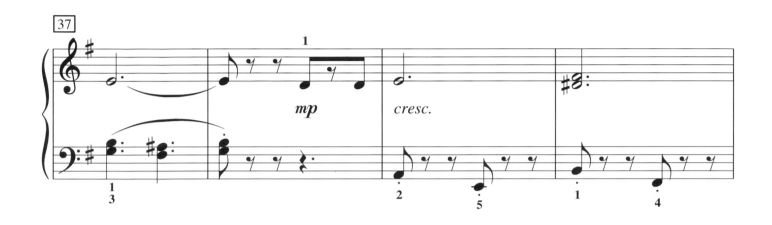

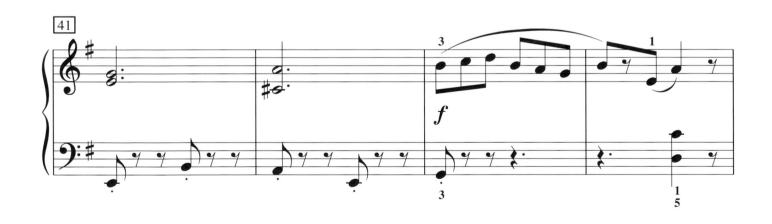

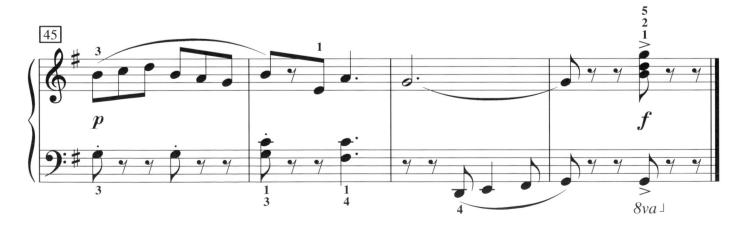

26

It's Beginning To Look Like Christmas

* 12/8 is like two measures of 6/8

Moderately

Words and Music by
Meredith Willson

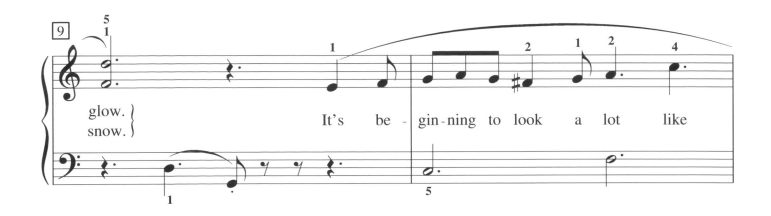

glow. / snow. It's be - gin - ning to look a lot like

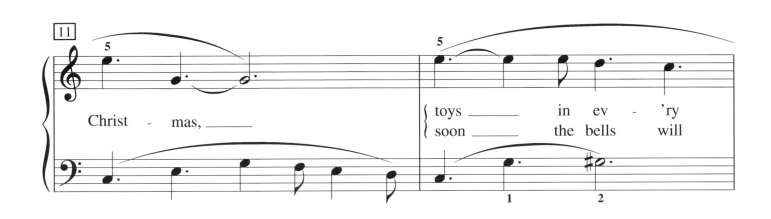

Christ - mas, _____ toys _____ in ev - 'ry / soon _____ the bells will

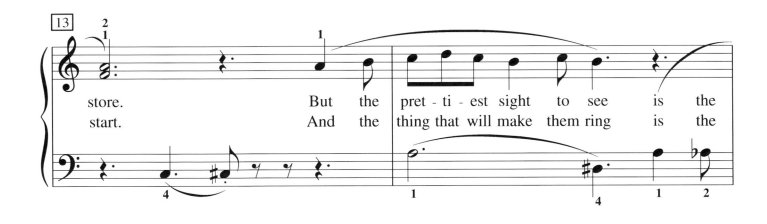

store. / start. But the / And the pret - ti - est sight to see is the / thing that will make them ring is the

To Coda ⊕

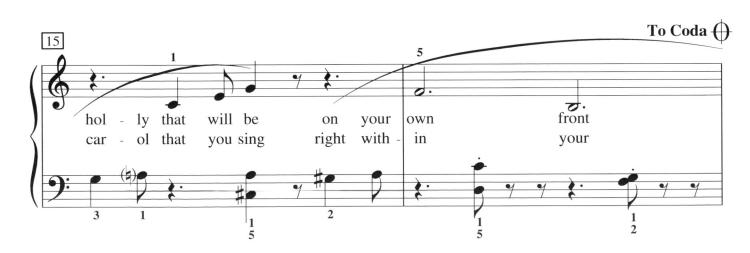

hol - ly that will be on your own / car - ol that you sing right with - in your front

door.   A   pair   of   hop - a - long boots and   a   pis - tol that shoots is   the

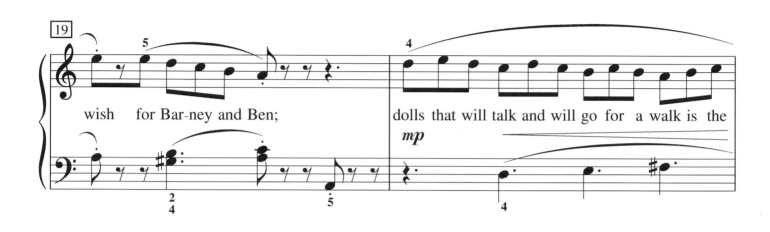

wish   for Bar - ney and Ben;   dolls that will talk and will go for   a   walk is   the

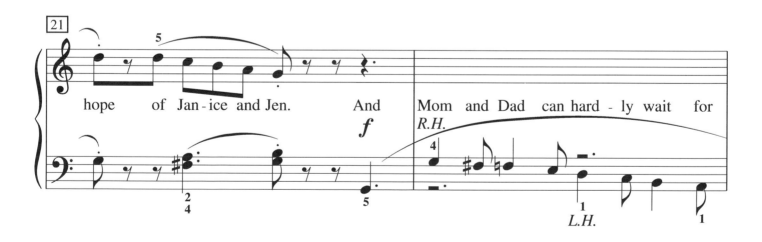

hope   of   Jan - ice and Jen.   And   Mom   and   Dad   can hard - ly   wait   for

D.S. al Coda

CODA

school   to   start   a - gain.   It's   be -

heart.

The Christmas Song
(Chestnuts Roasting On An Open Fire)

Music and Lyrics by Mel Torme
and Robert Wells

Chest-nuts roast-ing on an o-pen fire, Jack Frost nip-ping at your nose, yule-tide car-ols be-ing sung by a choir, and folks dressed up like Es-ki-mos. Ev-'ry bod-y knows a tur-key and some mis-tle-toe help to make the sea-son bright. Ti-ny tots with their eyes all a-glow will find it hard to sleep to-night. _____ They know that

Hal Leonard Student Piano Library

The *Hal Leonard Student Piano Library* has great music and solid pedagogy delivered in a truly creative and comprehensive method. It's that simple. A creative approach to learning using solid pedagogy and the best music produces skilled musicians! Great music means motivated students, inspired teachers and delighted parents. It's a method that encourages practice, progress, confidence, and best of all – success.

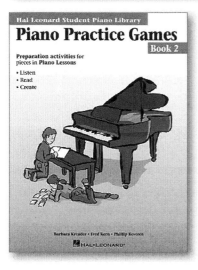

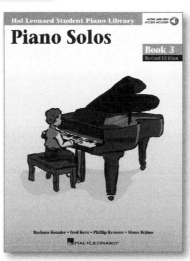

PIANO LESSONS BOOK 1
00296177 Book/Online Audio............................ $9.99
00296001 Book Only... $7.99

PIANO PRACTICE GAMES BOOK 1
00296002 .... $7.99

PIANO SOLOS BOOK 1
00296568 Book/Online Audio............................ $9.99
00296003 Book Only... $7.99

PIANO THEORY WORKBOOK BOOK 1
00296023 .... $7.50

PIANO TECHNIQUE BOOK 1
00296563 Book/Online Audio............................ $8.99
00296105 Book Only... $7.99

NOTESPELLER FOR PIANO BOOK 1
00296088 .... $7.99

TEACHER'S GUIDE BOOK 1
00296048 .... $7.99

PIANO LESSONS BOOK 2
00296178 Book/Online Audio............................ $9.99
00296006 Book Only... $7.99

PIANO PRACTICE GAMES BOOK 2
00296007 .... $8.99

PIANO SOLOS BOOK 2
00296569 Book/Online Audio............................ $8.99
00296008 Book Only... $7.99

PIANO THEORY WORKBOOK BOOK 2
00296024 .... $7.99

PIANO TECHNIQUE BOOK 2
00296564 Book/Online Audio............................ $8.99
00296106 Book Only... $7.99

NOTESPELLER FOR PIANO BOOK 2
00296089 .... $6.99

PIANO LESSONS BOOK 3
00296179 Book/Online Audio............................ $9.99
00296011 Book Only... $7.99

PIANO PRACTICE GAMES BOOK 3
00296012 .... $7.99

PIANO SOLOS BOOK 3
00296570 Book/Online Audio............................ $8.99
00296013 Book Only... $7.99

PIANO THEORY WORKBOOK BOOK 3
00296025 .... $7.99

PIANO TECHNIQUE BOOK 3
00296565 Book/Enhanced CD Pack $8.99
00296114 Book Only... $7.99

NOTESPELLER FOR PIANO BOOK 3
00296167 .... $7.99

PIANO LESSONS BOOK 4
00296180 Book/Online Audio............................ $9.99
00296026 Book Only... $7.99

PIANO PRACTICE GAMES BOOK 4
00296027 .... $6.99

PIANO SOLOS BOOK 4
00296571 Book/Online Audio............................ $8.99
00296028 Book Only... $7.99

PIANO THEORY WORKBOOK BOOK 4
00296038 .... $7.99

PIANO TECHNIQUE BOOK 4
00296566 Book/Online Audio............................ $8.99
00296115 Book Only... $7.99

PIANO LESSONS BOOK 5
00296181 Book/Online Audio............................ $9.99
00296041 Book Only... $8.99

PIANO SOLOS BOOK 5
00296572 Book/Online Audio............................ $9.99
00296043 Book Only... $7.99

PIANO THEORY WORKBOOK BOOK 5
00296042 .... $8.99

PIANO TECHNIQUE BOOK 5
00296567 Book/Online Audio............................ $8.99
00296116 Book Only... $8.99

ALL-IN-ONE PIANO LESSONS
00296761 Book A – Book/Online Audio $10.99
00296776 Book B – Book/Online Audio $10.99
00296851 Book C – Book/Online Audio $10.99
00296852 Book D – Book/Online Audio $10.99

Prices, contents, and availability subject to change without notice.

www.halleonard.com

0419
024